THREE KEYS TO POSITIVE CONFESSION

THREE KEYS TO POSITIVE CONFESSION

by
Frederick K. C. Price, Ph.D.

Faith One Publishing
Los Angeles, California

Unless otherwise indicated, all Scripture quotations are taken from the *King James Version* of the Bible.

Three Keys to Positive Confession
ISBN 1-883798-05-1
Copyright © 1994 by
Frederick K.C. Price, Ph.D.
P.O. Box 90000
Los Angeles, CA 90009

Published by Faith One Publishing
7901 South Vermont Avenue
Los Angeles, California 90044

Contents

Introduction

To most people, the word *confession* suggests admitting something we have done wrong: sin, wrongdoing, failure, or mistakes. However, in the context of the New Testament, it simply means to say the same thing God says, or to agree with what God says about you in His Word. It may include confessing sin, if you have committed it, but the word means so much more than that.

Every child of God needs to know how to make the right kind of confession, and to make it a part of his everyday life. This is because a person's confession will ultimately control his or her life and life-style. The right kind of confession will affect one's life in a positive way. The wrong kind of confession will just as surely ruin his life.

These are not just facts. They are spiritual laws. In fact, the law of confession is probably the single most important law you could ever learn about, because it is all-inclusive. It not only touches every area of life, but it actually dominates all of life. Indeed, a person's confession ultimately controls one's life and life-style.

That is why it is so important to learn how to make the right kind of confession — *positive confession* — and to know what the keys are for operating in it. It does not matter how much you may believe in faith, in healing, in prosperity. If the words that come out of your mouth on an everyday basis do not line up with what you profess to believe, you might as well throw in the towel right now, because you will not get any further along in the things of God than you are right now.

God has already given us the victory in all things through Jesus Christ. To put that victory to work for us, and to keep it working, however, we must learn to consistently say the things that keep God's power moving in our lives. That is what makes or breaks Christians in the things of God.

1

"Out of the Abundance of the Heart the Mouth Speaketh"

O generation of vipers, how can ye, being evil, speak good things? for out of the abundance of the heart the mouth speaketh.

(Matt. 12:34)

Your heart is your spirit. You are a spirit. You have a soul, and you live in a physical body. You are a tripartite creature. In other words, you are composed of three parts. With those three parts, you actually contact three worlds. With your spirit, you contact the world, or realm, of God. Jesus says, in John 4:24, **"God is a Spirit."** Genesis 1:26 says, **"And God said, Let us make man in our image, after our likeness...."** If God made us in His image, then we must be like God. God is a Spirit. Therefore, we also are spirits.

Genesis 1:26 could not be talking about our being made physically in God's image. If we looked like God physically, then God would be a monstrosity. He would have a white face, a black body, red arms, brown legs, and yellow feet, because those are the five major classifications of mankind on the earth. That would be ridiculous. God is a Spirit, so when Genesis says that

1

we were made in God's image, it means we were created as *spirits*.

When the Bible speaks of the heart, it is not talking about the muscle that pumps blood through your body. The Bible often uses the word *heart* figuratively, referring to the center or core of your being. When we talk about the heart of a melon, the heart of a tree, or the heart of a problem, we are talking about the center and core of those things. When the Bible talks about the heart of man, it is talking about the center and core of man. What is man at his center or core? He is a spirit. When the Bible talks about your *heart*, therefore, it is really talking about your spirit.

With this information in mind, read Matthew 12:34 once more, and let me point out something of the utmost importance to us as Christians.

> **O generation of vipers, how can ye, being evil, speak good things? for out of the abundance of the heart** [or the spirit] **the mouth speaketh.**
>
> **(Matt. 12:34)**

In other words, out of the abundance of your spirit, your mouth will speak. If your mouth is not speaking right, therefore, something must be wrong with what is inside of you.

Someone may say, "Well, Brother Price, the Lord knows I have a praise in my heart, and that I don't do much talking." The Lord also knows that person just lied. The Bible says, **"For out of the abundance of the heart the mouth speaketh."** If the mouth is not speaking, it must be because there is nothing in the heart.

2

We can, therefore, measure a man's spirit by his mouth. Of course, we should live right, and act right, but sometimes people can fool you with their actions. They can seem to be one thing, and can actually be something else. Sooner or later, however, their mouths will give them away, because their mouths will speak what is in their hearts. If you have an evil heart, you cannot speak good things.

Jesus amplifies this concept still further in verses 35 through 37 of Matthew 12:

> **A good man out of the good treasure of the heart bringeth forth good things: and an evil man out of the evil treasure bringeth forth evil things. But I say unto you, That every idle word that men shall speak, they shall give account thereof in the day of judgment. For by thy words thou shalt be justified, and by thy words thou shalt be condemned.**
> **(Matt. 12:35-37)**

The word *idle,* in verse 36, means useless, negative, non-productive. In other words, idle words are words that have no value; they do not edify you or build you up. They do not do any good for you. And, according to Jesus, we have to give an account of those words in the day of judgment: **"For by thy words thou shalt be justified, and by thy words thou shalt be condemned."**

Isn't it interesting that Jesus does not say we are justified or condemned by our *deeds,* but by our *words*? That is an awesome statement. The reason Jesus says, **"By thy words,"** is that your deeds will be based on your words. Ultimately, if you continue talking badly, you are going to act badly. If you keep talking sickness, you will have sickness. Keep talking failure, and you will fail.

We can see very clearly here how important our words really are. We not only affect our lives by what we say, but we are also judged by it. By our words, we can either be justified or condemned.

What You Believe, and What You Say

Another reason we have to measure what we say is explained by Jesus in Mark 11:23:

> For verily I say unto you, That whosoever shall say unto this mountain, Be thou removed, and be thou cast into the sea; and shall not doubt in his heart, but shall believe that those things which he saith shall come to pass; he shall have whatsoever he saith.
>
> **(Mark 11:23)**

Jesus says, **"For verily I say unto you, That whosoever shall say...."** You cannot say anything without words, so Jesus is talking about speaking or saying something.

He continues, **"... and shall not doubt in his heart,"** (or in his spirit), **"but shall believe...."** Where should you believe? In your heart. It is not stated directly here, but we can infer that if God does not want doubt in your heart, then your heart must be where He wants the belief.

"...and shall not doubt in his heart, but shall believe that those things which he saith shall come to pass; he

shall have whatsoever he saith." Even though what a person has said may not have come to pass, he should continue to believe that what he says shall come to pass. Jesus does not say that such a person has a 60-40 chance of getting it, or that it depends on the weather conditions. He said, **"He shall have whatsoever he saith."**

Read Mark 11:23 once again. This time, I would like you to notice a mathematical equation in that verse that shows us how important saying what we believe really is.

> **For verily I say unto you, That whosoever shall say unto this mountain, Be thou removed, and be thou cast into the sea; and shall not doubt in his heart, but shall believe that those things which he saith shall come to pass; he shall have whatsoever he saith.**
>
> **(Mark 11:23)**

The word *believe* is used only once in this verse. However, the word *say*, or some variation of it, is used three times. Believing is important, because believing is what we start out with. But if you believe without saying anything, you will not get what you believe, and it will not affect you in a personal way.

Many people believe many things, and some of these people believe the right thing, but they still do not have very much in their lives, and they wonder why. In many cases, it is because they are not saying anything. They do not understand the principle of confession — the principle of saying with your mouth what you believe in your heart.

Some of these people think it is dishonest to say you have something when you do not physically see it. They do not understand that, in Mark 11:23, Jesus is talking about a faith transaction. He says, **"... and shall not doubt in his heart, but shall believe...."** He does not say to have it, see it, or feel it. He says to *believe* it. He tells us, **" ... believe that those things which he saith shall come to pass...."**

You Are What You Say

Whether you realize it or not, you are the sum total of all you have been believing and saying about yourself all your life. We say so many things sometimes that we are totally oblivious to what we say about ourselves. Many people have talked themselves into sickness, into poverty, into fear and lack, and they have not realized it. They thought as long as they believed right, they could say whatever they wanted with their mouths, and the believing still would work.

That is not true.

Believing and saying go together. Consequently, what you say is what you get. You mark the person who consistently talks negativism, and you will see a person with negativism in his life. If you want things to start getting better, start lining up your heart and your mouth with God's Word. When you do that consistently, you will begin to produce in your life the things the Word declares.

Believing in your heart and confessing with your mouth are divine principles. In Romans 10:10, Paul uses salvation as an example of how this principle works:

> **For with the heart man believeth unto right-eousness; and with the mouth confession is made unto salvation.**
>
> **(Rom. 10:10)**

You can drop the word *righteousness*, insert anything else in there that you want, and the principle will still work. It always works, just as surely as two-plus-two always equals four.

Let us say, for example, you want to be physically healed. The principle is: For with the heart man believes in physical healing; he believes that by Christ's stripes he has already been healed, and with his mouth, he makes confession unto it by saying, "I believe I am healed." That is what will make physical healing become manifested in your life.

Your mind will not agree with this principle, however, unless it has been renewed by the Word of God. You have to reprogram your mind with the Word — then you can grasp it. Some people do not understand this, and because they are trying to grasp the principles of faith with their unrenewed minds, their heads block them from receiving God's best.

With the Head, or With the Heart?

When you are believing with your head, you need some kind of physical evidence to support your belief.

7

You need to see, touch, or hear something before you can give full credence to what you want to believe.

Actually, what you see around you is irrelevant, because the things you see around you always change. I have driven in some parts of a city where I saw a filling station located on a particular corner one week. The next week, there was nothing at the same corner except a hole in the ground. Bulldozers had removed the building in short order. If you had been planning your entire game plan according to that filling station, your whole game plan would now be changed, because that filling station was removed. It is no longer there.

When you are believing with the heart, you go by only what is written in the Word of God. You operate independent of what you see around you. In fact, what you see may contradict what the Word says, but if you are believing with the heart, that will not matter. You will know in your spirit that God said it, you believe it, and that settles it.

For example, let us say you are not feeling quite right one morning. You are feverish, you ache all over, and you feel miserable. The doctor checks your pulse, takes your temperature, and tells you that you are sick. Your head will remind you of what the doctor said — that you have a temperature of 105, and that you could do yourself some harm if you get out of bed. But your heart will tell you that you do not care what the temperature is, that the Word of God governs you, and that the Word says that with Jesus' stripes, you were healed.

This is not Science of Living, Science of Mind, or any of the other mind-science religions. They will tell you that you really are not sick They will tell you there is no such thing as illness, that it is something in your mind. Faith does not say that. It simply gives credit to the cure, rather than to the illness.

Faith must make the choice between the symptoms and God. Faith does not say you are not hurting when you are in pain. It does not say there is no temperature. If those things were not real, 1 Peter 2:24 would not say that by Christ's stripes, we were healed; and Matthew 8:17 would not say, **"Himself took our infirmities, and bare our sicknesses."** *Sickness and disease are real.*

However, what faith does is confess the Word instead of what your body is telling you. Instead of saying, "I have a temperature of 105, I ache all over, and I feel terrible," faith says, "I believe I am healed, in Jesus' name."

"What should I do about my feelings then, Brother Price?" If you are going to believe with the heart, you should ignore them. Do not pretend they do not exist, but concentrate instead on God's Word.

In the beginning, walking by God's Word can be frightening, because it defies all logical processes of reason. Spiritual things do not make sense, intellectually. You have to determine whether or not you will go through with your commitment to walk in the Word. In many respects, this is like jumping off a diving board. You have to make up your mind, because once you leave the board, there is no turning back. The next stop is the water. Before you jump, you have to make a commitment. It is either the board or the water. You cannot have them both.

Believing Is Not Feeling

Some people say, "I know I'm believing with the heart when I *feel* like I'm believing it." They think they are being spiritual when they have some kind of emotional response, but that is an even bigger mistake than believing with your head.

There may be some feelings involved when you experience the things of God, but your feelings really have nothing to do with the things themselves. If you allow your feelings to be the gauge by which you determine where you are with God, the results can be disastrous.

That is how many people mess up in marriage. A man and woman will live together five, ten, twenty years, then get a divorce because they "do not love one another anymore." The reason they do not love each other, as it turns out, is that they do not have the same emotional feeling for one another that they used to have.

It is to be expected after many years of marriage that you will not have the same feelings for one another that you had before. It was infatuation that you felt when you were courting one another. Sure, there should always be feelings involved, but love is more mature than fickle feelings are, and it goes deeper than the level of emotions. If your love is based solely on infatuation, you will be up the creek, in a boat with no oars, when the feelings of infatuation wear off.

Walking in the things of God is similar to marriage in some respects. As it is with marriage, measuring the things of God by your emotions can be deceiving. Many people doubt their salvation because getting saved was a very emotional experience for them. The grass looked greener, the sky looked bluer, and the person was on "cloud nine," and still ascending. After a while, that euphoria wanes, and everything becomes, for want of a better word, routine. Because it seems routine, it does not seem real anymore.

Many churches stress the emotional aspect. Everyone feels good when the service is over, but they do not learn anything about the Word. Essentially, all they get is a sweet pill of emotion. That sweet pill is what Satan wants them to go on, because he knows that if they get one sweet pill of emotion every week in church, and they do not get the Word, he can govern their lives through their emotions the other six days of the week.

When the devil comes in the midnight hour, you had better know more than "Jesus, Jesus, Jesus," and "Glory, glory, glory!" The devil will not run from that. He will stay right there and stomp you to death, if you let him.

I cannot say this enough: *Learn to walk according to the Word.* That is how you will know you are believing with the heart. Your heart will always take the side of God's Word. When you do that, you will have a joy that so transcends any emotional experience that there will be no comparison. That is how it should be with the mature Christian. Your feelings will fluctuate with the weather, but the Word of God always stays the same.

Once you start walking by the Word, it may take awhile before what you are believing for physically becomes manifest, because it takes some time for your confession of faith to take root in your heart realm, and for it to really begin to work. Not only that, but you have an opposing force — Satan and his demons — trying to keep you from getting the things you desire. The devil will try to use reasoning and emotions to force you to stop using your faith.

However, you can plow right through what Satan and his forces throw at you when you walk according to the Word of God. Jesus says that the person who says with his mouth, and believes with his heart, shall have whatsoever he says. Do not go by what you feel, but go by what God says in His Word.

Your Tongue Controls Your Life

We read that out of the abundance of the heart, the mouth speaks. We read that if you believe with the heart, and confess with your mouth, you shall have what you say. Another very important verse on confession is Proverbs 18:21:

Death and life are in the power of the tongue: and they that love it shall eat the fruit thereof.

There is a very important spiritual law connected with this verse, as there is with the others we have read in this chapter. If you can remember this law, and make it part of your daily life, it will guarantee your success.

The law I am referring to is this: *Your faith will never rise above the level of your confession.* In other words, your faith is governed by your confession. If you confess doubt, that is where your faith will operate — at the level or in the area of doubt. Your words will determine where your faith operates.

There are people who are not even Christians who operate by this law. They make it a point to say only positive things, and they are the most successful people in business, in finance, and in many other areas. They are still going to hell, but they are going as millionaires.

You may say, "I'd rather go to heaven poor than go to hell rich." Fine. That is your privilege. But why not take full advantage of your covenant rights? Follow this law, become successful, and go to heaven.

The reason most Christians are not as successful as they could be is that they talk themselves right out of it. They will say, "Praise the Lord! I have great faith," but if you ask them if they are sick, they will immediately answer, "Yes."

These people do not realize that is where their faith is operating. They confess they are sick, they believe in sickness, and they are having exactly what they say. It does not matter how much they say they have faith. As long as they confess the opposite of what God says about them in His Word, they will have exactly what they are saying in their lives.

What you have to do is to bring your confession up to the level of God's Word. When you do that, your faith will operate on the level of God's Word.

I started bringing up my confession to the level of God's Word years ago. Prior to that time, I had always struggled, financially. I was a preacher, had been a preacher, and did not love the Lord any less, but nothing was working for me. Every week was a struggle. Sometimes, I became so frustrated that, because I knew

I would not have anything left, I would say, "I am going to get myself something before those people get my money!" I would go out, and add something else onto my charge account, and did not realize that I was only digging my hole deeper.

Then I began to find out about the principles of faith. I began to find out that my faith would never rise above the level of my confession. And I found out that, as long as I confessed lack, want, and inability, that was what I would have in my life.

Instead of these negative confessions, I started confessing what the Word said. I started confessing that God was my Source. I began to confess that all my needs were met, in the name of Jesus. Physically, they were not met. But I began to say that I was not going to add anything else onto the charge accounts, and that I was going to believe God. If we did not have the money, we were not going to get anything. I confessed that we were getting out of debt, and that we were free.

I hooked my mouth up to my heart, and I hooked my heart to the Word. It took some time before I saw any tangible results, but eventually, because I kept confessing it, and because I got my life in line with the Word, and started tithing, I got out of debt, and now I walk in abundance. I am free!

It is absolutely thrilling to know my need is met, that all the bills are paid. But the way I got into this freedom was with my mouth. The more I confessed it, the more I saw myself with no financial need, with money in my pocket, and money in the bank — and this was long before it physically manifested.

Standing Against Attacks

While you are believing with your heart, and confessing with your mouth, the enemy is going to attack you. All of us can be attacked, no matter how long we have been living by the Word. In fact, the more you get in line with the Word of God, and the more of a threat you become to the kingdom of darkness, the more attacks Satan will lay against you in order to try to keep you from influencing others about the things of God.

Let us go back to sickness for a minute. Satan can only influence you by symptoms, through your body and your mind. He will bring a symptom to you, and he will immediately send a thought to your mind about it.

Here is where the battle is won or lost. Right at the moment that thought hits, you can side with the symptoms, or you can side with the Word of God. Whichever one of those things you side with is the one that will be confirmed in your life. God does not confirm anything but His Word, so if you decide against His Word, God cannot help you. He wants to help you, but He will not do it if you will not let Him by your words. By your confession, you control God's influence on your life.

I mentioned earlier that your faith will never rise above the level of your confession. That is a spiritual law. Another spiritual law that is just as important is this: *sickness confessed is sickness possessed.* If you confess the sickness, you will have sickness. If you believe it, and confess it, you will have it.

On the other side of the ledger, we see that the Word of God confessed is the Word of God possessed. When the enemy attacks my body, the first thing out of my mouth is not, "Oh, I'm sick! I guess I'm going to have another cold." The first thing that pops out of my mouth is, "With His stripes, I was healed." That is the first thing I do. I confess out loud that I believe I am healed.

The more you get into the Word, the more you find out who you are in Christ. When you find out who you are, the attacks become nothing more than a nuisance factor, and you handle them in the same way you would flick flies. But to do this, you have to learn how to confess the Word.

Do Not Guess How God Will Do It

One of the areas in which we miss out with God is when we try to figure out how God is going to impact our lives. We have a habit of reducing God to the level of human understanding and logic. We may look at the mountain of our financial situation, or whatever else it might be, and we cannot figure out any way under heaven to handle it. Since we cannot figure it out, we assume there is no way God can do it either.

When we do this, we cheat and rob ourselves. We should not be interested in how God is going to do something. What we should concentrate on is keeping our faith on the line that what we are believing for is done, in Jesus' name.

I am really never interested in how God does something. I know that Philippians 4:19 says, **"But my God shall supply all your need according to his riches in glory by Christ Jesus."** I do not care if He sends a collie down the street with a brown paper bag in his mouth with $1,000 in it. He can have a helicopter fly over my house, and drop it in the back yard. How God gets the money to me is His part, not mine. My part is to do what He tells me to do.

If I believe that God is meeting my needs, I cannot and should not sit around thinking, "Suppose this does not work? Where am I going to get the money?" When you do that, you disqualify yourself, because you nullify your own faith.

If you are going to believe the Word, you have to make a confession consistent with it, and stick with it. When your mouth lines up with the Word of God, that puts God to work on your behalf. When your mouth goes contrary to the Word, however, God does not have anything with which to back you up.

Positive Confession Is a Habit

If we desire to walk in victory every day of the year, we must form the habit of making a positive confession whenever we speak. Most people think of something bad when they see or hear the word *habit,* but there are really more good habits than there are bad ones. It is a good habit to bathe, to brush your teeth, to comb your hair, and to use deodorant. Another good habit is to continually confess the right thing.

Somehow, we have gotten the idea that when you get into spiritual things, if you do anything on a routine basis, it is not spiritual. For something to be spiritual, it has to be done on an impulse, just like the song, "Every time I feel the Spirit moving in my heart, I will pray."

That means if you do not feel the Spirit moving, you will not pray. They treat reading the Bible, giving the offerings, and other things of God the same way.

This is a big mistake!

You must learn how to do things in the spirit life just like you do things in the physical life — in other words, on a consistent, routine basis. It does not take anything away from them because you are doing them regularly. If anything, it reinforces those things in your life, and gives you a greater benefit from them than if you do them piecemeal.

I have a daily routine that you could set your watch by. After I get up in the morning, and go to the potty, I go back to bed, and pray for an hour and thirty minutes — first an hour in tongues, praying in the spirit, then about twenty to thirty minutes in English. When I finish praying in English, I wait awhile, and ask the Lord if He has anything He wants to say to me. If He does not speak, I say, "Praise the Lord. Thank you."

There is also a certain amount of Bible reading I do every day. The minimum that I set for myself is five chapters a day, mostly out of the New Testament (although I read from the Old Testament regularly as well). I do that simply to keep my eyes, my mind, and my spirit exposed to the Word. I read for that purpose, just to keep my spiritual muscles nimble and toned in the same way you condition your physical body with exercise. Sometimes I read more than five chapters, but that is the minimum I set as a goal for myself. If something comes up, and I miss out on my Bible reading for one day, I double up on the amount I read the following day.

You may think that all that prayer and Bible reading is bondage, but it is no more so than brushing my teeth, or combing my hair. I would not waste my time combing my hair if I did not like the way I looked after doing it. In other words, combing my hair is of benefit to me.

We should transfer this principle to our lives when it comes to spiritual things. Form the habit now of confessing with your mouth what God says, because when you do so it is of benefit to you.

"But, Brother Price, I don't know too much about the Bible." You will be at a serious disadvantage in that case, so start learning now. "Yes, pastor, but they don't teach the Bible at my church." That tells me that you are going to the wrong church. Find a church that teaches the uncompromising Word of God, and start attending.

"But I do not know where to go to church. Will you pray with me that the Lord will show me which church to go to?" No! If you have to pray about what church to go to, you are already in such bad shape that prayer is not going to help you. You do not have someone pray with you about where to buy gasoline or groceries. You generally go where you get the best deal for your money.

This should be what governs where you go to church as well. Go where you are "getting the best deal for your money" — where you can be taught the Word, and where the power of God is in operation. Go where God is moving, where the people are being changed for the better.

Mark 16:17-20 tells us,

> **And these signs shall follow them that believe; In my name shall they cast out devils; they shall speak with new tongues; They shall take up serpents; and if they drink any deadly thing, it shall not hurt them; they shall lay hands on the sick, and they shall recover. So then after the Lord had spoken unto them, he was received up into heaven, and sat on the right hand of God. And they went forth, and preached every where, the Lord working with them, and confirming the word with signs following. Amen.**

God does not confirm preachers. He does not confirm denominations. He does not confirm church buildings or choirs. He confirms the Word, and He does so with signs following. What kind of signs? Any kind you can think of: miracles, healings, deliverance, demons cast out, people getting saved and filled with the Spirit, lives brought back together, homes brought back together. When a church gives the Word, God will honor it.

God does not limit himself to churches. When you as an individual give the Word, God will move fast! We need to learn to make a habit of saying the kinds of things that will bring God's presence upon our lives and upon our circumstances. How is this done? By operating in the three keys to positive confession we will learn about now.

2

Guard Your Mouth and Your Mind

The first key to positive confession is: *We must learn to guard our mouths and our minds.* This is what David talks about in Psalm 141:3, when he says, **"Set a watch, O Lord, before my mouth; keep the door of my lips."** Here, David is asking God to do it. Keep in mind, however, that every time you ask God to do something, He puts the ball back into your hands, so that you can put what you ask into operation. God will tell you and show you how to do it, but you are the one who is responsible for the doing.

Your mouth is hooked up to your mind. When your mind gets messed up, your mouth gets messed up also. When you straighten out your mind, your mind will control your mouth. Ideally, your heart or your spirit should control your mind and your mouth. However, you have to progress to that point, and that will take some effort on your part.

> **I said, I will take heed to my ways, that I sin not with my tongue: I will keep my mouth with a bridle, while the wicked is before me.**
>
> **(Ps. 39:1)**

21

Notice the word *will*. It indicates a volitional act on the part of the individual. In essence, it says I am going to watch my ways, so that I will not sin with my mouth. The way by which I will not sin is by putting a bridle in my mouth. That is a drastic action. When you put a bridle on a horse, that bridle has a bit in it to help control him. If you want him to go to the right or to the left, you pull on the bridle in the direction you want to go, and it makes the horse pull his head that way so he will go in that direction. He has to go that way in order to keep the bit from hurting him.

This is what David is talking about doing when he says, **"I will keep my mouth with a bridle, while the wicked is before me"** (Ps. 39:1). He is talking about doing this not only around people, but around wicked people — namely, people who are influenced by Satan and demons. Satan and demons are around all the time, so you need to put a bridle on your tongue.

Some of the biggest problems you have gotten into have been because of your mouth. You said something, then regretted the fact that you said it almost as soon as it left your mouth — especially when you got into trouble because of it.

You are responsible for what comes out of your mouth, and out of your mind. Jesus says we will be either justified or condemned by our words. He also tells us, **"Out of the abundance of the heart the mouth speaketh"** (Matt. 12:34). Faith is released by what you say, so the words you speak will indicate the level of faith you are exercising. You need always to speak faith-filled words, words that will enhance, build up, and edify your faith, and make it strong.

Guarding Against "Corrupt Communication"

You must also guard yourself against saying things that are negative, or things that are in opposition to the Word of God. Whenever you say anything that is opposed to the Word of God, God cannot operate on your behalf. In either case, you are in control of your words, and your words control what happens in your life. Ephesians 4:29 tells us the following:

> Let no corrupt communication proceed out of your mouth, but that which is good to the use of edifying, that it may minister grace unto the hearers.

"Let no corrupt communication proceed out of your mouth." This means corrupt communication cannot come out unless you allow it to. The fact that you can allow it to come out means you are in total control of your mouth, and you are totally responsible for what comes out of it.

It also means you have the power to choose words that will enhance your life, instead of words that will destroy it. *Corrupt* (in the original Greek) literally means unedifying, useless, of no value. You have the ability to use words that are edifying, useful, and of great value to force a positive outcome in your life.

Many people have prospered, and did not know why. They thought they were lucky. However, if you examine their lives, you will find they were people who always talked in positive ways. Spiritual laws work, whether or not you know they are working, just like the law of gravity always works without your knowing its intricacies. The glorious news is that you can know that spiritual laws are working, and you can control them so that they can work on your behalf. That is the privilege God has given to us.

Are Unspoken Thoughts Dangerous?

Paul tells us not to let any corrupt communication **"proceed out of your mouth"** (Eph. 4:29). There is an implication here that is at least as important as the fact that you can control your mouth. The implication is that if a corrupt thought enters your mind, it is not really dangerous until it proceeds out of your mouth.

Satan has tricked many people with an age-old ruse. That ruse is, *it is just as bad to think it as it is to say it.* This is the biggest lie he ever told, and it is a trap he will try to use on you. You should know your own heart. You should know that you do not want to think anything filthy, unkind, or unpleasant, yet once in a while, a thought like that will enter your mind. I do not care who you are. It happens to everyone.

The reason it happens is that your mind is open both to Satan and to God. Satan *cannot* force you to do anything against your will, and neither *will* God. God has made us free moral agents, and He has given us the privilege to make choices. He *will not* violate our free will, and neither *can* the devil. However, they can influence you one way or the other.

Satan will try to influence you by planting thoughts in your mind. You can always tell when a thought comes from the devil, because that thought will always be inconsistent with and contradictory to the Word of God. You can ask yourself, "Does this thought edify? Does it build me up? Does it make me better for it? Does it make me freer than I already am? Does it reveal the mind of God to me?"

Satan is very clever at his job. He has learned not only how to plant thoughts in our minds, but he has also learned how to govern us in such a way that will make us think we engendered the thought. That way, we will take responsibility for it, and feel guilty because of it.

It is really not the thought that is important. It is what you do with it. That is what determines what your life-style is going to be. If you entertain that thought, and you begin to believe it and confess it, it will eventually govern your mind and your life. Satan will remind you, "Well, you know that it is just as bad to think it as it is to say it. Since you thought it, you might as well say it."

That is not true!

The truth is, any thought in your mind that is never uttered will die unborn. It is when you speak it out that the thought receives power and life. Therefore, if it is not a right thought, do not say it.

This does not mean that you can sit around and think about all sorts of ungodly things. Do not fall into that trap. The point is, do not let Satan put you in bondage, and make you give up on trying to do the right thing, simply because he has implanted a thought in your mind. Forget that thought. Kick it out like a computer kicks out wrong information. Transfer it out by replacing it with a corresponding thought that is consistent with the Word of God.

Get to Know the Word

This places a great responsibility upon you to know what is in the Word. Some people complain that they cannot understand the Word. Actually, the reason they do not understand it is that they do not spend any time in it.

We talked in the last chapter about how we should make positive confession a regular habit, something we do all the time, every day. We should also do that with studying the Word. Many people make the mistake of putting spiritual things last, at the end of the day, after they have done everything else. When they do this, they end up not praying, not reading the Bible, and not studying the Word.

Put God first. The two most important things you can do any day in your life are prayer and reading the Word. In fact, it is more important to feed your spirit than it is to feed your body, because if you have an overweight body and a malnourished spirit, you will be in sad shape. That body will not do you any good when it comes to spiritual things. However, if you have a well-developed spirit, you are a blessing going somewhere to happen.

The more you study the Word, the easier it will become to do so, and the more you will receive from it. You will not understand any book if you do not read it.

When you go to school, the teacher gives you a text-book, and at first, you do not understand anything in it. However, as you study it, do research, go to class, and hear the lectures, what that textbook contains becomes clearer as time goes on. After a while, you have mastered it. The same thing applies to the Word of God.

Why would God give us something we could not understand, especially when it is something we are supposed to use to live by? That would be the silliest thing in the world for Him to do. You can understand God's Word, but it will cost you some time, effort, and energy. God's Word is like a gold mine — the riches are there, but you have to dig for them. If you want to succeed in life, and walk above sickness, disease, want, and worry, it is easily worth the time you spend in the Word.

One thing that hangs many people up is that they are so busy criticizing others, and worrying about what they have, that they permit resentment to get into their thinking. They begin to operate in resentment and jealousy, and when you do that, you have hanged yourself.

When you speak, God hears what you say. That includes your criticism. This is why Ecclesiastes 5:2 tells us,

> **Be not rash with thy mouth, and let not thine heart be hasty to utter any thing before God: for God is in heaven, and thou upon earth: therefore let thy words be few.**

I am never concerned about what anyone else has. No matter what you have, I am not going to get jealous over it. If I see you with something, it lets me know two things. First, it lets me know it is available. Second, it lets me know that if you can have it, so can I.

Do not worry about whether or not you have five cars to drive, six houses to live in, or that you have super joy all the time. If someone has it, it must be available, and that means you can get it, too. That is the joy of it — that there is more than enough for all of us.

There is no need to wonder and find fault, if I decide to buy myself a second house, live in it one week, and live in the other one the next week. That is not all there is to life, but it is a part, and I have to sleep somewhere at night. It is better to sleep in a nice, comfortable bed, in a room with beautiful draperies on the wall, and lush carpet to walk on, than it is to sleep on a dirt floor. If you like dirt floors, help yourself, but the Bible says that these are the things God, the Father, has available for us.

Learn to Listen to Yourself

Again, we are told, **"Be not rash with thy mouth"** (Eccles. 5:2). In other words, learn to control your mouth. Why? Because your mouth is speaking forth what is inside of you. Therefore, what you speak is going to control your life.

This means we must learn how to listen to ourselves. Most people really do not hear what they are saying; they need to discipline themselves in order to hear their own words. This is one of the problems that crops up in marriages; many times, husbands and wives do not communicate with each other. Instead, they talk *at* each other. They bounce words off of each other's eardrums, but they never really hear what the other person is saying.

Until you learn how to govern your talk, and how to be consciously aware of what you are saying, you can get yourself in considerable trouble by saying the wrong thing. As I pointed out in the last chapter, the reason why many Christians are poor, sick, and defeated is that they talk themselves into those things. If they listened to what they said, they would be very careful to say things which were consistent with God's Word.

In James 1:22-24, there is a truth I want us to notice. It shows us how much we really do not listen to ourselves:

> **But be ye doers of the word, and not hearers only, deceiving your own selves. For if any be a hearer of the word, and not a doer, he is like unto a man beholding his natural face in a glass: For he beholdeth himself, and goeth his way, and straightway forgetteth what manner of man he was.**

Whether it is to shave, comb your hair, put on makeup, or just to see who is staring back at you in the morning, you have many occasions to look at yourself in the mirror. In fact, if you added up all the times you looked at yourself, it could possibly total into the thousands of times.

With that in mind, let me ask you a question: How long is your nose?

Chances are that your answer is, "I don't know." That is because you have never taken the time to measure your nose.

How do you measure your nose? You take a ruler, and place it next to your nose. You measure your words the same way — by placing the "ruler" of the Word of God next to them.

Once you start doing this, you will be amazed at how critical you become about your own words. You will begin to search your heart, and find out what it contains. When you start listening to your words, you will be amazed at some of the things that come out of your mouth. But once you do all this, you will bring your confession in line with the Word, and once this happens, you will start living. Jesus says:

> **For verily I say unto you, That whosoever shall say unto this mountain, Be thou removed, and be thou cast into the sea; and shall not doubt in his heart, but shall believe that those things which he saith shall come to pass; he shall have whatsoever he saith.**
> **(Mark 11:23)**

He says you will have not just what you say, but *whatsoever* you say. That includes sickness, disease, poverty, fear, depression, inability. You name it, and you will have it, if you continue believing and confessing it.

Every time you open your mouth and let a word out, you energize it. That word becomes powerful. A word is of no importance or value until it is spoken. Once you speak it, you put energy into it, and you cause it to start working. If it is a negative word, it will work against you. If it is a positive word, consistent with the Word of God, you put God to work on your behalf.

Bound in Body, Bound in Mind

Many people are so bound in their minds it prevents them from receiving the things of God. Because their minds are bound, their words are bound. Because of this bondage, these people do not bring their thoughts into line with God's Word, and they bring their own physical bodies down to the level of sickness and disease.

We must learn how to refuse everything that is of a negative, depressing, or resentful nature. As I mentioned earlier, your mind is open to the influences of Satan. He can drop a thought into your mind, just as God can drop a thought there. It is what you do with the thought that makes the difference.

This is why Proverbs 4:23 tells us, **"Keep thy heart with all diligence; for out of it are the issues of life."** We could read it this way: Keep thy heart with all discipline. We have to discipline and guard our hearts, and allow those things which are consistent with God's plan and purpose for our lives to come into it.

Proverbs 30:32 adds this instruction:

> **If thou hast done foolishly in lifting up thyself, or if thou hast thought evil, lay thine hand upon thy mouth.**

The verse does not say, "If thou hast said evil." It says, **"If thou hast thought evil."** Your thoughts are not conceived in your mouth. They are conceived in your mind; they come out of your mouth, and they filter into your spirit. Yet this verse tells us, **"If thou hast thought evil, lay thine hand upon thy mouth."** This is because, as we pointed out before, if the thought in your mind is left unsaid, it will die unborn.

You can have a fifty-gallon drum of the best corn seed, and if you do not do anything with it, that seed will sit in the drum and do nothing, even if you leave it there for ten years, or twenty years, or longer. That seed has all the potential that is necessary for a harvest. However, it will never do anyone any good until it is planted in the ground. When the seed comes into contact with good soil, all things being equal, it will germinate and produce a harvest.

Your words in your mind are like the seeds in the drum. If you keep those words in your mind, they will never produce anything, either positive or negative, in your life. The minute you vocalize those words, you have planted some seeds, and you have a harvest coming, good or bad, positive or negative. This is why the verse says, **"If thou hast thought evil, lay thine hand upon thy mouth."** When you confess that word, that is when you have the power working behind it.

I said this before, but it bears repetition, because it is of such vital importance to us. Satan has no entrance to your life, except through your thoughts. It is also the only way God can get into your life. God will try to influence your thoughts, and get you to act on them. Once you act on them, you come into contact with His power and His will.

Satan works the same way, only his aim is to destroy our lives. He gets his kicks out of making us hurt, and he has a great number of people hurting over all kinds of things. But the only way he can get to you is through your thoughts. That is why it is so imperative to guard our minds and our mouths, and why 2 Corinthians 10:3-5 tells us the following:

> For though we walk in the flesh, we do not war after the flesh: (For the weapons of our warfare are not carnal, but mighty through God to the pulling down of strong holds;) Casting down imaginations [literally, reasonings], and every high thing that exalteth itself against the knowledge of God, and bringing into captivity every thought to the obedience of Christ.

You get the knowledge of God from the Word of God. What Paul is saying is that we are able to govern every thought that comes into our heads. We are able to examine those thoughts, and we are to discipline our thought lives to the extent that when a thought comes into our minds that is contrary to the Word of God, we cast it down, or throw it away. That is our responsibility.

The exciting thing about this verse is that it says we have the ability to do that. It is nice to know that someone cannot come and push something off on us against our will. We have to consent to it for it to work either for us or against us. We are in control.

How will you know if a thought is contrary to the knowledge of God? By reading and studying the Word. Get the Word into you. Build it into your spirit, so that when these thoughts come, you can immediately submit them to the knowledge of God, and deal with them accordingly. That is what Paul is getting at in Romans 12:2, when he tells us,

And be not conformed to this world: but be ye transformed by the renewing of your mind, that ye may prove what is that good, and acceptable, and perfect, will of God.

Your mind is the gateway to your spirit. The things you hear enter your mind, and they eventually filter down into your spirit. If you do not have the right thing in your mind, you will have the wrong thing in your spirit. When you have the wrong thing in your spirit, you will have the wrong thing coming out of your mouth. And when you have the wrong thing coming out of your mouth, you are going to get the wrong thing in life. It is all tied together.

For this reason, God wants us to renew our minds. We do that by programming our minds with the Word, by building the Word into our minds, instead of building in the ways we did in the world. It takes time, energy, effort, and discipline, but the benefits you receive as a result of it are well worth all the effort.

... that ye may prove what is that good, and acceptable, and perfect, will of God.

(Rom. 12:2)

34

I used to think there was only one place in the Bible where God challenges us to prove Him, and that was relative to tithing in the Book of Malachi. But here is another place where God says to prove Him. How do you do that? By renewing your mind with the Word, and beginning to operate in line with that Word. When you put yourself in line with it, and begin to say what the Word declares, you will begin to see God moving on your behalf in your life.

For instance, the Bible says in Isaiah 26:3, **"Thou wilt keep him in perfect peace, whose mind is stayed on thee: because he trusteth in thee."** In John 14:27, Jesus adds, **"Peace I leave with you, my peace I give unto you: not as the world giveth, give I unto you. Let not your heart be troubled, neither let it be afraid."** If you want peace, you can have it. The Bible tells us that we can prove God, and have His peace.

Day after day, people come into my office whose heads have been "squashed" by the cares of life. They have no joy, no peace, and they say, "If I could just find some peace." I tell them that they can find it, but they are passing right by it. They are trying to find it in the bottle, in running after fourteen different women, in having fourteen men on the side. They are working themselves to death on their jobs, trying to get a lot of money in the bank, so they can have peace and happiness. Go, ask some of the millionaires out there — those who are contemplating suicide. They will tell you that money is not the answer!

You can have the peace of God, but you are going to have to have it on God's terms. You get it by programming your mind with the Word, and letting that Word proceed from your mouth. As you send that Word forth from your mouth, you create the reality of that peace around you.

God will mount guard around you with His angelic forces, and cause you to walk in peace, even when there is turmoil all around you. Everyone else in the office may panic, saying, "What will we do? We're getting laid off!" You just walk through the office, and keep saying, "My God shall supply all my need according to His riches in glory by Christ Jesus." (See Phil. 4:19.) Keep confessing it, keep your mind focused on the Word, and God will not only meet your need, but keep you in perfect peace while He is doing it.

3

Never Confess Doubt

Our second key to positive confession is this: *Never confess doubt, or anything else of a negative nature.* Admitting doubt, even in a small way, will paralyze your faith. It will have the effect of withholding God's best and His blessings from you. Therefore, we must never confess doubt.

I want you to notice how I phrased that statement. I said we must never *confess* doubt. I did not say you will not have doubt, or that it would never rear its ugly head. I said we must learn not to confess the doubt, because doubt confessed is doubt possessed. If you say it, you will have it.

Every one of us is subject to doubt. Satan, who is the instigator of doubt, will assail your mind with it from time to time. His purpose in doing this is to get you to question the truthfulness and accuracy of God's Word. If Satan can get you off of the Word, he has you in his hip pocket.

Many Christians become upset because they have doubt. They fall into condemnation, and think that God does not love them anymore, or think they are not operating in faith anymore — all because that doubt came to them. However, doubt comes to all of us. If doubt did not come, we would not know how to stand against it. You could lie down and believe, but Paul tells us in Ephesians 6:13-14,**"... and having done all, to stand. Stand therefore."** Why? Because you are going to be assailed by doubt, and doubt is the greatest enemy of God's Word.

I mentioned in the last chapter that when Satan shoots evil thoughts into your mind, that the thought itself is not important. It is what you do with it that determines how dangerous it is. The same is true for doubt. It is not the doubt that is important, but what you do with it.

What you should do with doubt is to *ignore it*! Doubt is real. It will come. But do not allow or permit it to have anything to do with your life-style, or with your making any decisions concerning the things of God.

God's Side, and Our Side

Too many Christians allow doubt to influence them, and that is where they get tripped up. They think, "Does God really mean what He says about...?" The answer to that question is, of course, He does. If God did not mean it, He would not have said it.

God will do exactly what He says He will do, but not until you do what you are supposed to do. There is a God-ward side and a man-ward side to every promise He has made to us, and God has already done His part. The Book of Hebrews says that God has rested from His labors. He is not doing anything today, because He has already put into operation everything that is needed for us to walk in salvation, to walk in power, and to be the Body of Christ in the Kingdom of God as we ought to be.

The Bible tells us to labor to enter into God's rest. The first thing we will run into as we start to labor to enter into it is doubt. Doubt will challenge you right at the gate.

For instance, some pain may come. Some people will tell you there is no such thing as pain, that it is all in your mind. If that pain is only in your mind, why is there a knot on your head the size of a lemon? That is not your mind. That is a tumor. To say you do not hurt when you are hurting would be telling a lie. The same goes for saying you are not sick when you are sick, or for saying there are no symptoms when there are symptoms.

What you should do is ignore the pain and the symptoms. When you do not want to be bothered with someone, you act like that person is not there. Do the same thing with the pain and the symptoms. Do not confess the pain, but confess the cure for the pain. Confess God's Word. When you do that, you will drive the pain out.

Confessing the pain will not get rid of the pain. It will only increase it, because pain confessed is pain possessed. Sickness confessed is sickness possessed. Fear confessed is fear possessed. Poverty confessed is poverty possessed. Inability confessed is inability possessed. When you say it, you will have it. That is what creates it for you.

This is why we need to learn what God says about these things. When the pain comes, what does the Bible say? It says that with Jesus' stripes we were healed. Therefore, it does not matter what the pain says. You are healed because of what the Word says. If you think that does not make sense, you are right. It is not sense. It is faith.

Again, ignoring the pain does not mean it does not exist. Pain exists. It is real. I have hurt to the point of screaming, so I know what pain is. Similarly, I have felt pain melt away like a snowball in the hot July sunshine when I have confessed God's Word instead of the pain.

It was a challenge to confess the Word, especially at first. It was much easier to say, "I hurt," than, "I believe I am healed," because I did not have any physical evidence that I was healed. I did not know that the Word of God was my evidence, and when you do not realize that, the Bible can seem intangible — just words on a page. However, this Word is real. It will work if you will get it into your heart, and let it come out of your mouth.

Waver, and You Will Not Receive

> If any of you lack wisdom, let him ask of God, that giveth to all men liberally, and upbraideth not; and it shall be given him.
>
> **(James 1:5)**

Here, James is using wisdom as an illustration, but in verses six and seven, he gives us a principle we can use not only with wisdom, but also in asking God for anything else:

> **But let him ask in faith, nothing wavering. For he that wavereth is like a wave of the sea driven with the wind and tossed. For let not that man think that he shall receive any thing of the Lord.**
>
> **(James 1:6-7)**

In short, if you waver, you will not receive anything. What does wavering mean? It is like a teeter-totter — sometimes up, sometimes down, sometimes hot, sometimes cold. It is never constant. The only way you can keep from wavering is by confessing only what the Word says, not your doubts.

Why does our wavering keep us from getting what we want from God? Is it that God withholds it from us when we waver? No. God does not withhold anything from you. There is really only one person who can keep God's blessings from you. That person is you. God has already put the blessings out there, but you are the one who has to get them. Ephesians 1:3 informs us,

> **Blessed be the God and Father of our Lord Jesus Christ, who hath blessed us with all spiritual blessings in heavenly places in Christ.**

All spiritual blessings include every blessing you could ever receive — a new car, a house, or whatever. "But, pastor, it says all *spiritual* blessings." I know it does. When the things come from God, they start out as spiritual commodities. It is your faith that causes spiritual blessings to be turned into physical and material ones. It is your faith that transfers them from the spirit world into the physical world.

This verse says we are already blessed. What we have to do is get the blessings, but we will never get them by wavering. As long as you are in a state of wavering, your faith will not be constant, and you will never bring anything to pass that you desire. Faith is a spiritual force, and it can move mountains. But like any other kind of force, it has to be constantly applied to the object it is standing against, or else that object will never move.

Walking by Faith Is Not Walking by Your Senses

Some people call walking by God's Word "stepping out on blind faith." Faith is not blind. Faith can see better than your eyes can. You can look at something with your eyes, and still not see what you think you are looking at. For example, there is false hair for men, elevator shoes to make you taller than you really are, as well as anything false you can imagine to make women more attractive. The point is, the things you think you see are not what you are really seeing all the time.

Faith never fails to see what is actually there, because faith is the eye of your spirit. When you operate by the spirit, through the Word of God, you will see exactly what God says you will see, and you will cause the thing you see with your faith to come into manifestation in your life. That is why Paul tells us:

For we walk by faith, not by sight.

(2 Cor. 5:7)

You will never succeed in the things of God as long as you remain focused on what you see with your eyes, instead of on what you see with your faith. The things you see with your eyes are there, and they are real, but you have to look beyond them.

Actually, the word *sight* in this verse is somewhat misleading. In the Greek, it is not limited solely to visual perception. It actually refers to the totality of our ability to perceive the universe and the environment around us — what we hear, taste, touch, and smell, as well as what we see. It is talking about sense-knowledge evidence, as opposed to revelation-knowledge evidence that we get from the Word of God.

This verse brings two factors into juxtaposition — the Word of God against what our senses tell us. We stand in the middle, between them, and we have a choice as to whether to gravitate toward the Word, or toward what our senses tell us. Since we live in a physical world, there are times when we have to walk according to our physical senses. However, when it comes to the things of God, we will never achieve what we want as long as we are bound by what our senses tell us. That is why we have to walk by faith, and not by sight, when it comes to walking by the Word.

Paul adds the following:

> **While we look not at the things which are seen, but at the things which are not seen:...**
>
> **(2 Cor. 4:18)**

Symptoms are things which are seen. They are things you can feel, touch, taste, see, or smell. However,

Paul tells us not to look at them. He tells us instead to look at the things that are not seen. We could easily put it this way: "While we look not at the things which are perceived by the senses, but at the things which are not perceived by the senses:..."

In other words, we can never appeal to our senses to find out where we are with God. We must always appeal to God's Word, because this enables us to look at the thing that is not perceived by our senses. The things of God are not perceived by your senses. They are perceived by your spirit. Your faith is the avenue that causes what your spirit sees through the Word to come into physical manifestation in your life, and it is the confession of your mouth that makes it manifest, by your saying it.

> **While we look not at the things which are seen, but at the things which are not seen: for the things which are seen are temporal; but the things which are not seen are eternal.**
>
> **(2 Cor. 4:18)**

The things which are not seen must exist. If they did not exist, you could not see them anyway. Not only that, but if they did not exist, they could not be eternal, because you cannot have eternal nothing. If these things are eternal, they must exist.

We have been bound by our physical senses, because we live in a sense-oriented world. If you destroy a person's five basic senses, he or she will never know anything about the universe around them. Such a man will not have any mechanisms by which he can

44

get information from his environment. However, when you learn how to walk by the Spirit of God, you learn how to be independent of what your senses tell you.

When Satan tries to attack me with illness, I never confess the symptoms, but I have them, just like you do. Satan never ceases to assail all of us. If this were not the case, the sixth chapter of Ephesians would not be necessary for the mature Christian.

The Bible does not make such a distinction between the baby Christian and the mature Christian, and it tells us to put on the whole armor of God, so we can be able to stand in the evil day, and having done all, to stand. It tells us to take the shield of faith, whereby we can quench all the fiery darts of the wicked. Why? Because the devil will throw some of those fiery darts at us, and it is faith that will quench them.

All those things the devil shoots at you are in the natural (the tangible or fleshly) realm. You have to learn how to ignore them, and to go by what the Word of God says. It will take some commitment on your part to do this, but it is worth it, because you will come out on top.

Jesus Walking on the Sea

In the fourteenth chapter of Matthew, we have a perfect example of how your senses can defeat you in the things of God. Jesus and the disciples had fed the multitudes who had come to hear Him. He went up a mountain to pray, and sent the disciples into a ship to cross the sea. We will pick up the story at verse 25:

> **And in the fourth watch of the night** [sometime between 3:00 and 6:00 in the morning] **Jesus went unto them, walking on the sea. And when the disciples saw him walking on the sea, they were troubled, saying, It is a spirit; and they cried out for fear. But straightway Jesus spake unto them, saying, Be of good cheer; it is I; be not afraid. And Peter answered him and said, Lord, if it be thou, bid me come unto thee on the water. And he said, Come....**
>
> **(Matt. 14:25-29)**

The fact that Jesus said "Come" implies two things. First, Peter had *permission* to come. This means it must have been the will of God for Peter to walk on the water. Second, it implies that Peter had the *ability* to walk on the water. If he did not have that ability, Jesus would have known that as soon as Peter stepped out of the boat, he would sink, and He would not have told Peter to come.

> **And he said, Come. And when Peter was come down out of the ship, he walked on the water, to go to Jesus. But when he saw the wind boisterous....**
>
> **(Matt. 14:29-30)**

The water represents the circumstances, what your physical senses tell you. As soon as Peter took his eyes off of the Word of God — Jesus — and put them on the circumstances, fear came in. When fear arrives, faith leaves.

> **But when he saw the wind boisterous, he was afraid; and beginning to sink, he cried, saying, Lord,**

save me. And immediately Jesus stretched forth his hand, and caught him, and said unto him, O thou of little faith, wherefore didst thou doubt?

(Matt. 14:30-31)

Why did Peter doubt? Because he looked at the circumstances, and he permitted what he saw to govern him. When he allowed the circumstances to govern him, he began to sink. All Peter had to do was to realize that Jesus was standing out there in the same wind, on the same water, and He was not sinking. If Peter had done this, he would not have continued sinking. Instead, he allowed the circumstances to come between him and Jesus.

Seen Things Change

There was another incident, when Jesus and the disciples were going across the water, and Jesus went to sleep. The Bible says that the winds came up, the waves rose, and the boat was almost totally filled with water. The disciples came and woke Jesus, and said, **"Master, carest thou not that we perish?"** (Mark 4:38).

The disciples were already confessing they were going to die, and their boat had not yet sunk. They confessed it because they thought it, and they thought it because they saw it. If Jesus had continued to sleep, they would have perished. Instead, Jesus woke, stretched, walked to the bow of the ship, and told the wind, **"Peace, be still"** (Mark 4:39). The wind ceased, and the sea calmed down.

Those winds were subject to change. So is every other thing you can perceive with your senses. This is why Paul tells us in 2 Corinthians 4:18, not to look at them. He says, **"... for the things which are seen are temporal** [or temporary]; **but the things which are not seen are eternal."** He does not say the things which are seen do not exist. If they did not exist, why tell us not to look at them? Those things are real. However, we should not let them influence us. No matter how bad a situation is, it is subject to change.

On the other hand, the things which are not seen are not subject to change, because God says in His Word that He does not change. That means Jesus is not subject to change, and neither is the Word. The wind raged while Jesus was asleep, but that was not the end of the issue. Jesus stood up and told the wind to change, and it changed.

This is why we need the Word in us. We need to take charge over the circumstances in our lives, and effect a change for the better. But you cannot do that until you get the Word into your spirit, and confess that, instead of confessing what you see and feel.

4

Harmonize Your Confession With God's

The third, and final, key to positive confession is, *We must learn to harmonize our confession with God's.* In other words, we need to find out what God's Word says about us, then bring our confession into line with His. If God says north, we cannot say south. If God says east, we cannot say west. If God says up, we cannot say down.

The reason why people make negative confessions is that they do not know what God says in His Word. They know what their church says, and what the preacher says, but they do not realize that not everything the minister says is what God says. It may sound spiritual, but that does not make it right.

You have to find out what the Word of God says about you. This is because God deals with us on the basis of our confession. If you do not bring your confession into line with what God says about you in His Word, you will never receive the manifestation of God's best in your life. Whatever words you give God are the words God can use to bring His power to bear in your life.

If — the Great Off-Switch of Faith's Confession

Many times, without realizing it, we make confessions that are inconsistent with the Word. If I say, "I prayed for the healing of my heart condition, and I hope that God will heal me someday, if it is His will," it sounds honest, and it sounds as if it comes from my heart. Most of us have made statements and prayed prayers that sounded like this. We have also wondered why God did not answer those prayers.

The reason our prayers were not answered is that our confession did not agree with God's Word. You may not realize it, but when you say, "If it be thy will," you are confessing that you do not know what the will of God is. If you knew what it was, you would not say, "If it be thy will."

Let me tell you why you prayed like that. Number one, you did so because you were never taught how to pray properly. Number two, you prayed like that because you heard some saint pray like that. Number three, deep down inside, you did not think you were really good enough for God to give you what you wanted, but you hoped that you would still get it. Therefore, you prayed, "If it be thy will," because you figured that would be an act of humility on your part.

What you did not realize was that when you said, "If it be thy will," you took a giant eraser, and erased everything you prayed prior to this conditional statement. That is why God could not answer your prayer.

You have to make sure your prayers and your confessions are consistent with the will of God. "Well, how can I know the will of God?" Read the Word!

God's will is revealed in His Word. There is nothing wrong with watching soap operas, talk shows, or comedy shows on television, but you will not find the will of God there. If you want to find the will of God, you have to get into the Word.

"But, Brother Price, you know that you can't understand the Bible." If that is the case, why does God instruct us, through the Apostle Paul, to do the following:

> **Study to shew thyself approved unto God, a workman that needeth not to be ashamed, rightly dividing the word of truth.**
>
> **(2 Tim. 2:15)**

He adds the following, in 2 Timothy 3:16 and 17:

> **All scripture is given by inspiration of God, and is profitable for doctrine, for reproof, for correction, for instruction in righteousness: That the man of God may be perfect, throughly furnished unto all good works.**

Isn't that something? God did not realize when He told us to show ourselves approved, and that all Scripture is given by inspiration of God, and is profitable, that we could not understand it. What do we need it for if we cannot understand it?

You *can* understand the Word, but you will not understand it until you crack it open, and look inside. Once you do this, and learn to rightly divide the Word of Truth, it will benefit you enormously.

Submitting Yourself to God's Word

One verse of Scripture which is very familiar to many Christians is James 4:7:

Submit yourselves therefore to God. Resist the devil, and he will flee from you.

There is a very important key here. Most Christians usually quote only the latter part of this verse. That is one reason why the devil does not flee from them when they resist him. They are resisting, but they have not submitted themselves to God.

You submit yourself to God by submitting yourself to His Word. God is not here visibly and physically, but His Word is. If you have respect for God, you will have respect for His Word.

There are some people that I hold in high esteem. I do not have to be around them. I do not even have to see them. All they have to do is write me a letter, and give me their word in it, and their word in a letter is just as valid for me as their physical presence would be. That is because I have respect for them. I not only believe that the person is right, but also that his or her word is right. If I can believe that person, I also must believe his or her word.

We should treat God the same way. If you have great respect and love for God, you should also have great respect and love for His Word. You have never seen God, but God has manifested himself to you in His Word. If you believe God, you also have to believe His Word.

When you believe God, and submit to Him by taking Him at His Word, you can resist the devil, and he will flee from you. Resisting the devil also means resisting the symptoms when he attacks you with sickness. If the pain comes, and you say, "I rebuke you, pain, in the name of Jesus," and the pain does not leave, maybe it is not leaving because you have not submitted yourself to God.

The word *submitted* means to take direction from the person or thing you are submitted to. When you are submitted to God, you are giving precedence to His Word over the circumstances. When you give the Word precedence, and stand against that symptom by confessing what the Word says about it, that symptom will go away. However, if you allow that symptom to govern you, and you are in rebellion against the Word of God, you can say anything you want, and it will not work for you.

Building Up a Faith Vocabulary

Being submitted to the Word is a life-style. It is something you should do every day, not just when you feel like it. You cannot confess the Word one day, and the circumstances the next. You should always confess the Word. In order to do this, you must build up a vocabulary of faith, based on the Word of God.

Your vocabulary consists of the words you use in your life-style. Some people have a four-letter vocabulary. All they know how to say is a conversation full of profanity, because their vocabulary is limited to that. When you get into the things of God, you need to develop a Word-oriented vocabulary. You get that vocabulary from the Word of God. Build it into your spirit and your mind, and it will affect what you say with your mouth. When you do that, you will have God working on your side.

Many Christians defeat themselves because they build a vocabulary of doubt, based on what the world says, instead of a vocabulary that is based on God's Word. The Bible calls Satan "the god of this world." When these Christians say what the world says, they put Satan to work in their lives, without realizing it. He causes all the trouble, then lies to them, and tricks them into thinking that God is the one who is doing it to them. They ask, "Why did God do this to me?" when God was not the one who did it. They did it to themselves, with their own mouths.

You control God's power in your life with your words. You control your destiny. You are the captain of your own ship. We read in Proverbs 18:21 that life and death are in the power of the tongue, and they that love it shall eat the fruit thereof. Therefore, it is up to you to put God's power to work in your life by using a vocabulary of faith, instead of a vocabulary of defeat.

Sickness and disease are cases in point:

When the even was come, they brought unto him many that were possessed with devils: and he

54

cast out the spirits with his word, and healed all that were sick: That it might be fulfilled which was spoken by Esaias the prophet, saying, Himself took our infirmities, and bare our sicknesses.

(Matt. 8:16-17)

Why did Jesus take our infirmities, and why did He bear our sicknesses? He did this so you would not have to. Some people think God uses sickness and disease to chasten them, and make better people out of them. If the Lord wanted to do that, why would He say in His Word that Jesus took our infirmities, and bore our sicknesses, then turn around and require you to take and bear them? That would be counterproductive. Jesus took our infirmities, and bore our sicknesses, so we could be free!

"By His Stripes ..."

Another Scripture that talks about sickness and disease is 1 Peter 2:24:

Who his own self bare our sins in his own body on the tree, that we, being dead to sins, should live unto righteousness: by whose stripes ye were healed.

It does not say you are going to be healed. It says you were healed. If you were healed, that means you are well. The circumstances may say you are sick, but God's Word says you are well. You have the choice of either agreeing with God's Word, or agreeing with the circumstances. Whichever one you agree with is the one that will work on your behalf.

People have had the erroneous idea over the years that when Jesus went to Calvary, He trudged up the hill with a big bag of sins, went up to the cross, and nailed the contents of the bag up there. That was the idea I had in earlier years, but the Bible does not portray that at all. The Bible says that Jesus was made to be sin.

> **For he [God] hath made him [Jesus] to be sin for us, who knew no sin; that we might be made the righteousness of God in him.**
>
> **(2 Cor. 5:21)**

Jesus did not just take your sin and carry it. He was *made* sin with your sin, and then took the sin to the cross, and nailed it there. He took it out of the way, and that is what set you free. At the same time Jesus did this, the Bible says that with His stripes you were healed.

What does it really mean to say that by His stripes we were healed? When Jesus was arrested in the Garden of Gethsemane, He was taken into custody by the Sanhedrin Council. That was the Jewish high tribunal, roughly equivalent to the U.S. Supreme Court, and they took Jesus into custody because they did not like what He was doing. He was doing too many things that contradicted their traditions, and when you go against some people's traditions, you have a fight on your hands.

However, the Jews at this time were under the rulership of the Roman Empire, and the Jews could not try a capital crime. In other words, they could not execute anyone. Therefore, they brought Jesus to the governor, Pontius Pilate, with trumped-up charges, to get him to issue the order of execution. When Pilate had Jesus in custody, he asked Him some questions, and Jesus did not answer. So Pilate had some of his soldiers take Jesus, and they did to Him what the Bible calls "scourging."

Scourging is whipping. That was the Romans' form of interrogation. They would put you down on your knees, stretch your arms out in front of you, and lay your back even with the ceiling. The Roman soldier would then pull out a scourge, which was a whip made of leather thongs, with little balls of lead that had crushed glass in them tied to the ends of the thongs, and he would beat the person with it. They would not just whip the person. They would whip him, then drag the whip across his back, and the little lead balls with the crushed glass would rip and tear the person's back apart. A capital crime was worth forty stripes, save one, meaning thirty-nine lashes of the whip.

They laid thirty-nine stripes upon Jesus. When 1 Peter 2:24 says, **"... by whose stripes ye were healed,"** it is important to realize that in those lashes of the whip God saw the sickness and disease of mankind transferred from mankind to the back of Jesus. With His back bleeding, ripped, and torn, Jesus went to Calvary, and He was nailed to the cross. When they nailed Him to the cross, they nailed your sin to the cross, and they also nailed your sickness and disease there. All the sickness and disease of mankind for all time and eternity was placed upon His body, and He was made sick with every disease at the same time, so that you could be free.

That is why I personally will not accept sickness and disease. When I think of the price Jesus paid for me to be well, I count it a slap in His face for me to turn over and let Satan put sickness and disease on me, especially when he does not have a legal right to do so. The only way Satan can do that is with my mouth, by my saying, "I'm sick." Instead of that, I say what the Word says: He took my infirmities, and bore my sicknesses, and by His stripes, I was healed. When sickness rears its ugly head, I take the Word of God, and kick sickness in the head, and say, "In the name of Jesus, I curse you, foul disease. I refuse to receive you!"

God's Medicine

Before I came into the knowledge that by Christ's stripes I was healed, I kept my medicine chest stocked with aspirin, codeine, and all kinds of cold medicines. I expected to get sick, because I thought God was the one who was making me sick. Now I take God's medicine. Man's medicine will help you only after you get sick. God's medicine will keep you from getting sick.

What is God's medicine? According to Proverbs 4:20-22, it is this:

> **My son, attend to my words; incline thine ear unto my sayings.**

Words are individual entities. When you have sayings, you are stringing words together to form a statement or declaration.

> **Let them** [those words and sayings] **not depart from thine eyes; keep them in the midst of thine heart. For they are life unto those that find them,...**

If you have to find them, a little searching must go on. They are not just lying there, to be kicked around like an old can. You are going to have to seek and to find. Knock, and the door will be opened. Hunger and thirst after righteousness, and you will be filled.

> **For they are life unto those that find them, and health to all their flesh.**
>
> **(Prov. 4:22)**

Flesh refers to your body. Also, if you have a Bible with a center reference mark, you will notice a little note stating that the word *health* in the original Hebrew is the word *medicine*.

God's Word is medicine for your body. It is God's medicine. I start each day by taking my dose of it. I start by praising God that He took my infirmities, and bore my sickness, and with His stripes, I was healed. I thank Him that He sent His Word and healed me. I thank Him that He heals all my disease, and delivers me from all my destructions, because I have been redeemed from the curse of the Law, which is poverty, sickness, and spiritual death.

59

I go on by praising God for saying that he that dwelleth in the secret place of the Most High shall abide under the shadow of the Almighty, that a thousand can fall at my side, and 10,000 at my right hand, but it shall not come nigh me. I thank Him for saying that no plague shall come nigh my dwelling, that He is the one who will take sickness out of the midst of me (See Ps. 91, Exod. 23). I thank Him that He shall fulfill the number of my days, because He is Jehovah-Raphah, the Lord who heals me.

That is why I am strong — because I take God's medicine, which is God's Word. I take it by speaking His Word with my mouth. I have to get the words into my heart, so I can let them out of my mouth. But once I get them into my heart, and let them out of my mouth, they are energized with the power of God, and they work against the filth, disease, and sickness that Satan would try to bring against me.

Positive Confession Means Positive Prayers

A positive confession has to extend even to our prayer lives, or we cannot expect God to answer our prayers. You can be just as negative in your prayer life as you can be in your ordinary speaking life. In fact, many people are very negative in their prayer lives without realizing it. One example of this, which we discussed earlier, is when you add, "If it be thy will," to a prayer of faith. That is a negative prayer. It is a prayer of doubt, and when you are operating in doubt, you stop the power of God from being manifested on your behalf.

That is an awesome concept. We are flesh-and-blood creatures. Most of us could not stop a man going full-speed on a bicycle. None of us can stop an automobile, or catch a bullet flying through the air. Yet we have the ability to stop the power of Almighty God.

Remember that God is a faith God. Hebrews 11:6 says that without faith it is impossible to please Him. If I get my faith in the wrong area — in other words, if I am operating in a negative faith — I will stop the power of God. You can have a room full of lights burning brightly because of the electricity going through them, but when you flip the switch that controls the power to the off position, you cut off the electricity, and those lights will all go out. When you pray a negative prayer, that flips the light switch of faith to the off position.

What you have to do is bring your prayers, as well as your ordinary conversation, in line with God's Word. When you do this, you will start praying positive prayers. You will make positive confessions, and you will thereby put God to work in your life.

There is a kind of prayer in which you can use, "If it be thy will." It is called the prayer of consecration and dedication. Let us say you have been called into ministry. You could pray, "Father, I know you have called me into the ministry, and I am willing to go wherever you want me to go. If it be thy will for me to go to South Africa, I will go. If it be thy will for me to go to Alaska, I will go. If it be thy will for me to go to South America, I am willing to go, in Jesus' name."

Can you see the difference between this kind of prayer, and a prayer for God to give you something? You cannot go to the Bible and find a Scripture that says,

"Fred Price, go to...." Therefore, when you pray the prayer of consecration and dedication, you have to say, "If it be thy will," because God's will is not made known to you in the Bible concerning things like that.

A Plan for Living — and Winning!

Other than when you have to pray a prayer of consecration and dedication, anything that has to do with your physical life, your soulish life, or your spiritual life is covered in God's Word. When you pray for God to give you anything or to do something in your life, you should always make sure your prayer agrees with that Word. Bring your confession into line with God's Word, and study, so that you can thoroughly know and understand the Word of God.

Many people do not understand that the Bible is God's plan for living, or that it covers every contingency that could arise in their lives. Most Christians know about salvation, but they think that once you are saved, you are supposed to just "tough it out," and after you die, things will be better. That is not what is portrayed in the Word. God has a plan in His Word for your life.

Do not misunderstand me. I do not believe that the Word teaches that on Thursday morning, October 1, you are going to have cantaloupe, a glass of prune juice, three cups of coffee, a glazed doughnut, three eggs, two strips of bacon, and one link of sausage. God does not care what you eat, where you live, or what kind of work you do, apart from calling a man to ministry.

However, God does have certain principles you can put into your life-style, so that whatever you do, you are the best at it. You can be the best custodian, the best airline pilot, stewardess, mother, or whatever you do for a living, if you will implement your life-style with the ingredients God has made available to you. It will make you a winner.

> **Fret not thyself because of evildoers, neither be thou envious against the workers of iniquity. For they shall soon be cut down like the grass, and wither as the green herb. Trust in the Lord, and do good; so shalt thou dwell in the land, and verily thou shalt be fed. Delight thyself also in the Lord; and he shall give thee the desires of thine heart. Commit thy way unto the Lord; trust also in him; and he shall bring it to pass.**
>
> **(Ps. 37:1-5)**

Here is a formula for living. You may have more confidence in the six o'clock evening news than you have in the Word of God, but the Psalmist tells us, **"Fret not thyself"** (Ps. 37:1). Nobody else can make you do it. It takes *you* to make you fret.

The Psalmist goes on to say, **"...because of evil-doers, neither be thou envious against the workers of iniquity. For they shall soon be cut down like the grass, and wither as the green herb."** Nobody gets away with doing wrong, so do not worry about it. Man pays every week, but divine judgment does not necessarily pay off every week. But I will tell you one thing — it will definitely, finally, pay off. Meanwhile, we are supposed to do this:

> **Trust in the Lord, and do good; so shalt thou
> dwell in the land, and verily thou shalt be fed.
> Delight thyself also in the Lord; and he shall give
> thee the desires of thine heart.**
>
> **(Ps. 37:3-4)**

You may want to succeed in this area of life. Some of you are burning the midnight oil, working eight hours a day, plus going to school full-time at night, so you can get a better job.

You are knocking yourself out, and you claim that you do not have time for God.

When you promote the Word of God, God will promote you. Do not let God be second in your life. Let Him be *first*. You may not appear to rise as fast as the person sitting at the desk next to yours, but I guarantee you that if you delight yourself in the Lord, you will rise higher than he will ever go.

Here is what will make the desires of your heart come to pass:

> **Commit thy way unto the Lord; trust also in
> him; and he shall bring it to pass.**
>
> **(Ps. 37:5)**

Commit God's Word into your spirit. Let yourself say, "I delight myself in the Lord. Praise God. He will give me the desires of my heart. I trust in the Lord with all my heart, and He shall bring it to pass." Confess this over your life, and God will do it.

Dwelling in the Secret Place of the Most High

> He that dwelleth in the secret place of the most
> High shall abide under the shadow of the Almighty.
> I will say of the Lord, He is my refuge and my
> fortress: my God; in him will I trust. Surely he shall
> deliver thee from the snare of the fowler, and from
> the noisome pestilence. He shall cover thee with his
> feathers, and under his wings shalt thou trust: his
> truth shall be thy shield and buckler. Thou shalt not
> be afraid for the terror by night; nor for the arrow that
> flieth by day; Nor for the pestilence that walketh in
> darkness; nor for the destruction that wasteth at
> noonday. A thousand shall fall at thy side, and ten
> thousand at thy right hand; but it shall not come nigh
> thee. Only with thine eyes shalt thou behold and see
> the reward of the wicked. Because thou hast made
> the Lord, which is my refuge, even the most High, thy
> habitation; There shall no evil befall thee, neither
> shall any plague come nigh thy dwelling.
>
> **(Ps. 91:1-10)**

That means sickness and disease will not come near your house, provided you dwell in the secret place of the Most High, and abide under the shadow of the Almighty.

> For he shall give his angels charge over thee, to
> keep thee in all thy ways.
>
> **(Ps. 91:11)**

You may have been afraid of flying on an airplane, of going outside at night, or of any number of other

65

things. Fear is a terrible thing; there is nothing worse than being afraid. But you do not need to be afraid: **"For he shall give his angels charge over thee, to keep thee in all thy ways."**

Every one of us has a guardian angel. That angel has been keeping you from getting your head blown off many times. He will keep you alive when you are a sinner, so that you can be saved. But this verse says you have angels, *plural*. Not only do you have angels, but the Bible says God will give His angels charge over you. That means He commissions them to mount guard over you.

However, the angels cannot do anything for you to the fullest extent possible unless you are willing to believe they are there, and count on and expect them to work for you. You have to dare to believe it, dare to take God at His Word, and dare to confess it. Once you do this, amazing things will happen:

> **They shall bear thee up in their hands, lest thou dash thy foot against a stone. Thou shalt tread upon the lion and adder: the young lion and the dragon shalt thou trample under feet.**
>
> **(Ps. 91:12-13)**

That means the devil, and every demon, will be under your feet.

> **Because he hath set his love upon me, therefore will I deliver him: I will set him on high, because he hath known my name. He shall call upon me, and I will answer him: I will be with him in trouble; I will deliver him, and honour him. With long life will I**

66

satisfy him, and shew him my salvation.
(Ps. 91:14-16)

Get this Word into you. Confess it, and dare to make it personal. Say, "I dwell in the secret place of the Most High, and I abide under the shadow of the Almighty. A thousand can fall at my side, and 10,000 at my right hand, but it shall not come nigh me, because I dwell in the secret place of the Most High." That is what makes it work, and it puts the power into operation in your life.

Forgetting Not These Promises

The first five verses of Psalm 103 tell us even more:

> **Bless the Lord, O my soul: and all that is within me, bless his holy name. Bless the Lord, O my soul, and forget not all his benefits: Who forgiveth all thine iniquities; who healeth all thy diseases; Who redeemeth thy life from destruction; who crowneth thee with lovingkindness and tender mercies; Who satisfieth thy mouth with good things; so that thy youth is renewed like the eagle's.**

He says your youth is renewed like the eagle's. I confess that every day. I am getting older chronologically, but I am getting younger on the inside. I am not going to dry up like an old prune. I am not going to be decrepit when I am 100 years old. I will be just as strong as I am now, preaching just as loudly with a voice as strong as mine is now, praise God! I am taking God at His Word for everything He lists in these verses — and you should do so, too. You should not settle for anything less than God's best.

Another Scripture we want to look at is Psalm 121:

> I will lift up mine eyes unto the hills, from whence cometh my help. My help cometh from the Lord, which made heaven and earth. He will not suffer [actually, this word means *allow* or *permit*] thy foot to be moved: he that keepeth thee will not slumber. Behold, he that keepeth Israel shall neither slumber nor sleep. The Lord is thy keeper: the Lord is thy shade upon thy right hand. The sun shall not smite thee by day, nor the moon by night. The Lord shall preserve thee from all evil: he shall preserve thy soul. The Lord shall preserve thy going out and thy coming in from this time forth, and even for evermore.

This means we have divine protection all the time. I want us to especially notice verse four:

> Behold, he that keepeth Israel shall neither slumber nor sleep.
>
> (Ps. 121:4)

Many people, including Christians, unfortunately do not understand this principle. They stay awake all night worrying, trying to figure out where they are going to get the money they need. They stay awake pondering how they are going to do this, or how they are going to do that. They worry about the kids. The kids went out with God, but the parents are letting the devil keep them awake with visions of the kids tearing up the car and themselves.

If these people understood the principle enunciated in this verse, they would not allow themselves to do this. If God is not going to slumber or sleep, He is going to be awake. If He is awake, there is no point of your staying awake, so why not get some rest? If you stay awake all night, you are wasting your time. Instead of worrying, why not confess that God is preserving you, that He is protecting your going out and your coming in, that He is on your right hand, and you shall not be moved? You can confess that for yourself and for your entire family.

When You Seek First the Kingdom

Jesus tells us the following:

Which of you by taking thought can add one cubit unto his stature? And why take ye thought for raiment? Consider the lilies of the field, how they grow; they toil not, neither do they spin: And yet I say unto you, That even Solomon in all his glory was not arrayed like one of these. Wherefore, if God so clothe the grass of the field, which to day is, and to morrow is cast into the oven, shall he not much more clothe you, O ye of little faith? Therefore take no thought, saying, What shall we eat? or, What shall we drink? or, Wherewithal shall we be clothed? (For after all these things do the Gentiles seek:) for your heavenly Father knoweth that ye have need of all

> these things. But seek ye first the kingdom of God, and His righteousness; and all these things shall be added unto you.

(Matt. 6:27-33)

If you are not careful, you may get the idea that God is telling us to never consider what we will wear, where we will live, or what we will eat. That would be foolishness. The point Jesus is trying to get us to see is that we should not make these things the reason for our living. With many people, that is their entire life-style. That is all they do, and they run from one thing to another.

As I said, Jesus is not saying for us not to be concerned about clothing, houses, and all that. Those things are fine, and He wants us to have them, but He wants us to put them in their proper order. He says, **"But seek ye first the kingdom of God, and his righteousness; and all these things shall be added unto you"** (Matt. 6:33).

Notice that the things are not added until after the seeking. Seek the Kingdom first, and then the things will come. Begin to confess that you are a seeker of the Kingdom of God first. Think about it, say it, and you will be surprised at how smoothly your life will begin to run.

One Final Rule

These are just a few of the countless promises God makes to the believer, which if faithfully confessed, will enable you to live victoriously every day of your life. However, let me give you one final rule: *God never works in advance of the level of your faith.* Therefore, if you do not give God your faith, He has no channel to get to you what you desire, and what He wants you to have.

There is only one person who can rob you of what belongs to you, and that person is you. Paul tells us, in Romans 8:28, **"And we know that all things work together for good to them that love God, to them who are the called according to His purpose."** In other words, the end result of all things for you, the person who is in Christ, will be for your good. God can make it work out that way, if you will confess it, and if you will believe it.

What I am talking to you about is something that *works.* Once you start using a vocabulary of faith, it will bring you joy, it will bring you peace, it will bring you health, and it will bring you prosperity in every area of your life. It will bring homes together. It will bring husbands and wives together, to the point where they can love each other, and they can know they are for each other. It will bring children and parents together. And it works for anyone who uses it.

For a complete list of books and tapes by Dr. Frederick K.C. Price, or to receive his publication, *Ever Increasing Faith Messenger*, write:

Dr. Fred Price

Crenshaw Christian Center

P. O. Box 90000

Los Angeles, CA 90009

Books by Frederick K. C. Price, Ph.D.

HIGH FINANCE
(God's Financial Plan: Tithes and Offerings)

HOW FAITH WORKS
(In English and Spanish)

IS HEALING FOR ALL?

HOW TO OBTAIN STRONG FAITH
(Six Principles)

NOW FAITH IS

THE HOLY SPIRIT —
The Missing Ingredient

FAITH, FOOLISHNESS, OR PRESUMPTION?

THANK GOD FOR EVERYTHING?

HOW TO BELIEVE GOD FOR A MATE

MARRIAGE AND THE FAMILY

LIVING IN THE REALM OF THE SPIRIT

THE ORIGIN OF SATAN

CONCERNING THEM WHICH ARE ASLEEP

HOMOSEXUALITY:
State of Birth or State of Mind?

PROSPERITY ON GOD'S TERMS

WALKING IN GOD'S WORD
(Through His Promises)

KEYS TO SUCCESSFUL MINISTRY

NAME IT AND CLAIM IT!
The Power of Positive Confession

THE VICTORIOUS, OVERCOMING LIFE
(A Verse-by-Verse Study of the Book of Colossians)

A NEW LAW FOR A NEW PEOPLE

THE FAITHFULNESS OF GOD

THE PROMISED LAND
(A New Era for the Body of Christ)

THREE KEYS TO POSITIVE CONFESSION

Available from your local bookstore

About the Author

Frederick K.C. Price, Ph.D., founded Crenshaw Christian Center in Los Angeles, California, in 1973, with a congregation of some 300 people. Today, the church numbers well over 14,000 members of various racial backgrounds.

Crenshaw Christian Center, home of the renowned 10,146-seat FaithDome, has a staff of more than 250 employees. Included on its thirty-acre grounds are a Ministry Training Institute, the Crenshaw Christian Center Correspondence School, the Frederick K.C. Price III elementary, junior, and senior high schools, as well as the FKCP III Child Care Center.

The "Ever Increasing Faith" television and radio broadcasts are outreaches of Crenshaw Christian Center. The television program is viewed on more than 100 stations throughout the United States and overseas. The radio program airs on approximately forty stations across the country.

Dr. Price travels extensively, teaching on the Word of Faith forcefully in the power of the Holy Spirit. He is the author of several books on faith and divine healing.

In 1990, Dr. Price founded the Fellowship of Inner-City Word of Faith Ministries (FICWFM) for the purpose of fostering and spreading the faith message among independent ministries located in the urban, metropolitan areas of the United States.